HAUNTED CANADA 3

MORE TRUE GHOST STORIES

PAT HANCOCK

SCHOLASTIC CANADA LTD.

Toronto New York London Auckland Sydney
Mexico City New Delhi Hong Kong Buenos Aires

Scholastic Canada Ltd.
604 King Street West, Toronto, Ontario M5V 1E1, Canada

Scholastic Inc.
557 Broadway, New York, NY 10012, USA

Scholastic Australia Pty Limited
PO Box 579, Gosford, NSW 2250, Australia

Scholastic New Zealand Limited
Private Bag 94407, Botany, Manukau 2163, New Zealand

Scholastic Children's Books
Euston House, 24 Eversholt Street, London NW1 1DB, UK

www.scholastic.ca

Cover photo: First Light/Heritage Image Partnership
Illustrations by Kara-Anne Fraser

Library and Archives Canada Cataloguing in Publication
Hancock, Pat
Haunted Canada 3 : more true ghost stories / Pat Hancock.
ISBN 978-0-439-93777-1
1. Ghosts—Canada—Juvenile literature. I. Title. II. Title: Haunted
Canada three.
BF1472.C3H3534 2007   j398.20971'05   C2006-906676-0

ISBN-10 0-439-93777-9

10 9 8   Printed in Canada   121   13 14 15

MIX
Paper from
responsible sources
FSC® C004071

To Katharine, Jennifer and Michael — a fan club of three who mean everything to me — and to Keira, our latest source of joy.

Photo Credits

INTRODUCTION

People who know I write books will often ask me, "So, what are you working on now?" Over the last few years, when I explained that I was looking here, there and everywhere for material for the Haunted Canada books, I was surprised at how many of them had a true ghost story to tell. "That's great," I'd say, thinking I might be able to include their story in one of the books. But when I started asking them how they were affected by their ghostly encounters — Were you terrified? Did you scream? Did you move out of the house? and so on — I soon realized that, in most cases, there wasn't enough to tell. And if they had had a really terrifying experience, they didn't want me to write about it because they were afraid people would think they were crazy or just imagining things.

So I've begun to think that more people than you might expect have seen, heard, smelled or been touched by some mysterious presence that they call a ghost. They just don't want to admit it, or to talk about what happened publicly. But some true ghost stories — haunting events experienced by ordinary, sane, truthful people — do get reported. Here are some of the scarier ones.

HAUNTED ROOMS FOR RENT

Toronto, Ontario

One chilly January day in 1886, a widow and her daughter moved their possessions into their new home. They were looking forward to living in the roomy upper-floor flat they had just rented in an old house on Gerrard Street in Toronto. The next morning they were moving their things out of the house as fast as they could carry them. Their first night there had been absolutely terrifying.

The first thing they noticed was how cold the place was, even though they had managed to get a good fire going in the fireplace. Tired, they snuggled under extra bedclothes and eventually fell asleep. But not for long. Just before midnight they were awakened by loud banging and slamming sounds downstairs. And then, even though their bedroom door was shut, a blast of wintry air blew through the room, lifting the blankets right off their bed. The mother went out into the hall and called downstairs to Mr. Farrel, the owner who lived on the lower floor, asking him to shut the doors. But he had no idea what she was talking about.

Worried that her imagination was playing tricks on her, the mother went back to bed, calmed her daughter down, and said they should try to get some more sleep. But sleep never came. A while later, a dark mysterious shape drifted over the bed, leaving them trembling with fear, as did the thumping footsteps they heard moving along the hall.

Mother and daughter clung to each other until dawn. Then they rose, got dressed, packed their bags and left, telling Mr. Farrel that nothing could make them stay another minute in the upstairs flat they had hoped to call home.

DREAM WARNING

Tagish Lake, Yukon

Tagish Lake is a long, narrow lake crossing the border between the Yukon and British Columbia. For hundreds of years, members of the Gwich'in Nation lived a nomadic life along its shores. Then gold was discovered at Bonanza Creek in 1896, and the Klondike Gold Rush began. Prospectors from the south started moving into and through the area. Today the Klondike Highway follows the western arm of the lake in the Yukon much as the prospectors did more than a century ago.

Although the lake is rather isolated, it made news around the world after a large meteorite crashed into its frozen surface in January of 2000. A local resident, Jim Brook, collected the 200-gram meteorite and other smaller pieces of space rock, and made them available to researchers. They were very excited by his find. The Tagish meteorite turned out to be the most pristine, or uncontaminated, meteorite they had ever analyzed — and it was the very first one they identified as having come all the way from a band of asteroids between Mars and Jupiter.

The lake had also caught the interest of UFO (Unidentified Flying Object) researchers. In the early 1970s three people — two men and a woman — reported seeing seven large, round objects moving slowly in the sky over the lake. One of the men took a picture of the mysterious, bright orbs, and the other sent the photo to weather officials in Ottawa in the hope of learning what the UFOs were. He was eventually told that any information about them was classified.

But the most unusual event reported about the lake made the news back in 1916, when a somewhat strange article appeared in the *The Nome Daily Nugget,* the daily newspaper at the time in Nome, Alaska. The article recounted how Don Mack, a mining engineer working in northern Canada and Alaska, had written to a woman named Ethel Williams to thank her for saving him from drowning in Tagish Lake.

In his letter, Mack explained that he had been crossing the frozen lake by sled with three Native men and a French Canadian when they decided to camp for the night on a small island. During the night Mack had a vivid dream in which a young woman appeared. She identified herself as Ethel Williams of Syracuse, New York, and she warned him not to travel in the direction he planned to go the next day — because the snow-covered ice there was dangerously thin. When Mack awoke, the other men were packing up and getting ready to set off again, so he told them about his disturbing dream and suggested they follow a new route. But they just laughed at him and set off as planned, leaving him to continue on his journey alone.

Tagish Lake in winter

Mack wrote that he had detoured around the dangerous area he had been warned about by the apparition and made it safely to Skagway, but the four other men never showed up. Worried, he organized a search party to go back and look for them. Several days later, he was both saddened and stunned when he found the missing men's canoes and some of their gear floating in the lake's icy waters — very close to the place he had been warned to avoid. Mack and the other searchers presumed the four had drowned. Their bodies were never found.

Back in his office in Juneau, Alaska, Mack couldn't get thoughts of his dream and his narrow escape out of his head. After doing some research, he learned that a young woman named Ethel Williams did indeed live in Syracuse, New York, and he couldn't resist writing to her. He wanted to thank her for saving his life. Someone in Ethel's family — perhaps Ethel herself — was so amazed when the letter arrived that it was reported to a local newspaper, and the article that appeared was eventually picked up by *The Nome Daily Nugget.*

Ethel had been astonished when she read the letter because she had never heard of Don Mack, or Tagish Lake, and she had absolutely no way of knowing the ice conditions there in the late fall. But apparently Mack had met her once — in a dream he would never forget.

NiGHT ViSiON

North Atlantic Ocean

In the 1930s Joseph Boyd, a sea captain from Yarmouth, Nova Scotia, told folklorist Helen Creighton about a dream that *he* would never forget.

He had been serving as his brother's first mate on a sailing ship bound for New York in the late 1890s when his brother told him about a frightening dream he had just had. In it, several sailors were tied to the rigging of a badly damaged, wave-swept ship, their hands out-stretched as if pleading for help.

Joe kept thinking about the dream as he went about the stormy morning's tasks. Finally, for no good reason he could think of, he made the tricky climb up the rigging and scanned the churning waves. To his amazement, off in the distance he spotted a foundering vessel with all but one mast gone, and with men with outstretched arms tied to the rigging.

Joe shouted out the order to change course and, after hours of hazardous manoeuvering, the crew of his ship managed to rescue sixteen sailors perilously close to death. And Joe was convinced they would have died if it hadn't been for his brother's dream.

Sadly, some members of the shipwrecked crew had been washed overboard when the storm's fury first hit. Perhaps the dream was a last desperate effort by the ghost of one of those drowned men to save his fellow sailors before he journeyed into eternity.

A DEADLY DRIVE

Fredericton, New Brunswick

The brutal murder of taxi driver Norman Phillip Burgoyne in January of 1949 sent shockwaves of horror through Fredericton, New Brunswick.

Just thirty-four years old when he was killed, Burgoyne was married and the father of three young children. His wife reported him missing when he didn't return home after answering a Friday night call for a taxi from the Canadian Legion Hall. Three days later his body was found stuffed into the trunk of his cab at the southeastern outskirts of the city, on Wilsey Road.

Burgoyne's killers had badly botched their efforts to conceal their crime, leaving behind plenty of clues to their identities, and it took police just a couple of days to find them. Rufus Hamilton, aged twenty-two, and his brother

George, twenty-three, were charged with the murder. During their trial, George told the court how Rufus had bludgeoned Burgoyne with a hammer. Then they had robbed him. The Hamiltons were found guilty and sentenced to death by hanging. Both sentences were carried out on the same day in July of 1949.

There are those who believe that the two young men, united by their deaths just minutes apart, remained together in the afterlife — and that their ghosts still haunt Fredericton. The Hammer Brothers, as they came to be known, have been reported wandering through some of the city's back alleys. They've also been seen thumbing a ride into town, but no one will stop to pick them up — especially not along Wilsey Road.

THE HOUSE OF SPIRITS

Cobourg, Ontario

MacKechnie House is a charming home surrounded by lush gardens on Tremaine Street in Cobourg, Ontario. More than one hundred and fifty years old, the mansion has been restored to its original elegance and is now a popular bed and breakfast known for serving fine meals. It's also known by some of Cobourg's older residents for having had a few supernatural guests.

These folks remember hearing the drone of bagpipes when they played in the house as youngsters, and a few actually saw the piper, nattily dressed in his kilt and shiny black shoes, standing on the stairs. A little girl has also appeared on the stairs before running away, as if playing hide-and-seek. And an otherworldly, elderly lady seemed to like rearranging or hiding items in the house, and has even tucked a few unsuspecting guests into bed at night.

Today, the owners of the bed and breakfast manor don't use stories about MacKechnie House being haunted to attract clients to the stately home — and they're quite comfortable living in the house themselves. Though they did sense the presence of ghosts in the beginning, they feel they have moved on.

But superstitious guests with active imaginations might want to spend a day or two enjoying more than the scrumptious food and royal treatment the bed and breakfast is known for. They might actually book a room in the hope that they could come away with a ghost story of their own . . .

MacKechnie House

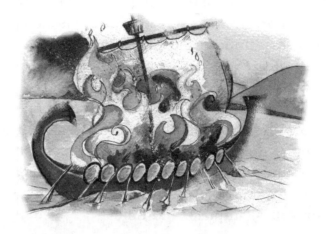

THE GHOSTLY GALLEY

Placentia Bay, Newfoundland

About 2800 years ago the Greeks and Phoenicians started building galleys — large ships propelled by oars — that were fast enough and strong enough to ram and sink enemy vessels. These warships had one, two or three rows of oars, powered by fifty, one hundred or one hundred and seventy men. With the oarsmen rowing steadily, galleys could maintain average speeds of about ten to fifteen kilometres an hour. Yet, no matter how well they rowed, even with the help of a single sail, they would not have set out to cross a large ocean like the Atlantic. They would have perished long before they reached the shores of Newfoundland.

But in the 1920s, centuries after these ships had disappeared into history, a galley suddenly appeared in

Placentia Bay, Newfoundland, to the west of the Avalon Peninsula. It was complete with a ghostly crew working two rows of oars. More terrifying still, the ship was on fire. People on shore spoke of how they could feel the fire's heat and hear the unbearable cries of the men aboard as flames engulfed the galley. And yet the ship sailed on until it suddenly vanished.

Back then, dozens of folks living in fishing communities around the bay reported sightings of the horrifying apparition. However, it has now been more than eighty years since anyone has seen the blazing vision and heard the mournful cries of the ghostly oarsmen who travelled so far off course in place and time.

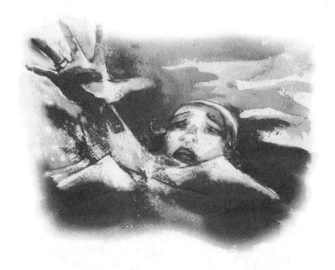

A GHOST ASKS WHY

Muskoka, Ontario

Jean Kozocari first saw a ghost in the 1930s. She was a young child at the time, spending the summer at her grandparents' riverside lodge in the Muskokas, Ontario's popular cottage country.

Two guests who had just arrived at the lodge were newly-weds. Competitive swimmers, they were honeymooning in the area so they could continue training for upcoming national trials. The day they decided to go for a swim was like so many others that summer — warm and sunny, with just a gentle breeze drifting through the trees. Other guests had warned the couple of a dangerous undertow in a turbulent section of the river, but they didn't seem concerned. They strolled down the path hand in hand, waded into the water until it was deep enough, and swam away.

Jean was playing outside then. She was still outside some time later — when the husband clambered back up the path gasping for breath and begging for help. People were shouting and running toward him. Jean was frightened. She was also confused. She could see guests rushing to put boats in the water when the frantic husband told them how his bride had disappeared in a swirling eddy and his desperate search to find her had failed. But Jean didn't understand — because she could also see his wife.

The young woman was standing near her husband. She was dripping wet, bent over slightly, and sobbing. And in the midst of all the noise and confusion, Jean could hear her moaning again and again, "How *could* you?" But people were still heading for the river to look for her and, gradually, it dawned on Jean that no one else could see her.

As dusk fell, the search was called off, and guests slowly returned to the lodge, talking in hushed tones about the missing bride. Her body was never found, but Jean saw her several times over the next few weeks, standing on a small island in the river, wet hair plastered around her face and doubled over as if in pain. And each time Jean saw her, she heard her cry out, "Why did he do it? I loved him."

Jean was too young at the time to make sense of what she saw that summer, but nearly fifty years later she would recall details of what had happened in *A Gathering of Ghosts*, a book she co-authored with Robin Skelton in which she described several other times she has seen, heard or sensed ghostly presences. The drowned bride was the first of many ghosts she would encounter over her lifetime, but memories of her often haunted Jean. Had the young woman's death been just a tragic accident? Or something much more sinister — a murder? Jean could never forget hearing her plead, "How *could* you?" that summer so long ago — nor stop imagining what she could have meant.

DEAD RED EYES

Clarke's Beach, Newfoundland and Labrador

Drowning claimed the life of another young woman whose spirit appears to have lingered after death. At least that's the explanation given for the terror three girls experienced at Clarke's Beach on the island of Newfoundland in the 1980s.

At the mouth of the North River, Clarke's Beach is one of several picturesque towns dotting the southwest coast of Conception Bay. The train no longer runs past the town, but part of the old railway bridge crossing the river is still there. That's where the teenagers were heading when they went for a walk one summer evening. It's also where they had the scare of their lives.

As they approached the span, the girls noticed a dark shape perched on it. Getting closer, they saw that it was a young woman in a bathing suit drying herself with a towel. She didn't seem to hear them coming. Wondering who she was, they took a few more steps toward her. Suddenly she turned and looked straight at them — and they froze in fright. Her eyes were glowing red like burning coals. Stumbling backward, the girls ran screaming from the bridge.

Several residents weren't too surprised when they heard about the spine-chilling apparition that had left the three teenagers so shaken. According to them, the girls hadn't been the first to report seeing the disturbing vision of the spooky female, and they might not be the last to do so, either. Some locals say she is the ghost of a young woman who, many years earlier, had gone to the bridge to meet her lover for a midnight swim. When he didn't show up as planned, she decided to go swimming anyway — alone. That decision proved fatal. But every now and then, she still returns — searching for her lover, probing the darkness with her glowing red eyes.

A FATHER'S FAREWELL

Near Fort Augustus, Northwest Territories

In the early 1800s, competition was fierce among fur trading companies operating in what would become Canada's prairie provinces and Northwest Territories. The Hudson Bay Company, the North West Company and the XY Company were busy building forts throughout the area — in hopes of attracting Native and Metis trappers eager to trade their furs.

James King was a trader for the North West Company operating around the North Saskatchewan River in 1802. That year his manager, John McDonald, asked him to go and meet with a group of Native people who had a large number of furs to sell. King had a reputation for being a tough man to deal with. Nevertheless, McDonald warned him to be careful of another rough and ready character named La Mothe, an XY Company clerk who was apparently going after the same furs.

King set out by sleigh from Fort Augustus, near the current site of Fort Saskatchewan, Alberta, telling his wife that he'd be back in three days. The second night he was gone, his six-year-old daughter woke, crying. When King's wife tried to comfort her, the little girl explained that she'd just seen her father near her in their tent — and that his neck was strangely red. After hearing her mother's reassuring explanation that the frightening vision had just been a bad dream, the girl went back to sleep. A few hours later, though, she was wide awake again, and she was very afraid. Her father, she told her mother, had returned. He had stood at the foot of the bed, watching her. And his neck was still all red.

The next day, King's wife told several people at the fort about what had happened during the night, and they all agreed with her that bad dreams had caused the girl such distress. They changed their minds, however, when the trading party returned with a sleigh loaded down with furs — and with the bloody body of James King. The night before, he had been in a fight with La Mothe, the XY Company's man. La Mothe had shot him through the neck.

Had James King's spirit returned that fateful night to spend a few final moments with his little daughter?

THE INVISIBLE FRIEND

Nanaimo, British Columbia

It's not unusual for a young child to invent an imaginary playmate. But when several children at a daycare centre in Nanaimo, British Columbia, started chatting with the same make-believe friend, caregivers wondered what was going on. A few youngsters even drew similar pictures of the mysterious child — in a white nightgown, playing with a red ball. Could it be that the children were seeing one of the spirits said to haunt Beban House?

Beban House was built in the late 1920s by Frank Beban, an immigrant from New Zealand who made his fortune in the lumber business. Beban moved into the impressive log mansion with his wife and four children in 1930, and lived there until his death in 1952. In 1953 the city of Nanaimo bought the house and the more than sixty hectares of Beban estate land surrounding it. Over the years the city put the property to good use, creating parkland and playing fields, and building a sports complex and other facilities used by various community groups.

But for four decades the mansion itself was largely neglected — until it was restored in the 1990s. In 1997 it became the new home to Nanaimo's tourism bureau. Before that a daycare centre had occupied the main floor. Some of the children attending the centre then, and several people who have worked in the building, appear to have one thing in common — an unexplained encounter with an eerie presence in the house.

Various organizations have offices in Beban House now, and some of their staff have reported unsettling experiences such as the sounds of dishes clattering in an empty room, water taps turning on mysteriously in a washroom, and cupboard doors and filing cabinet drawers flying open on their own. People have heard light footsteps scurrying up and down the stairs, and heavy footsteps stomping around in an empty room on the second floor. A woman has appeared suddenly in a hallway and then vanished as quickly as she came. And late at night when no one was in the building, passersby have seen a glowing light in the upstairs windows.

Frank Beban and his wife loved their beautiful home. Could it be that they have been reluctant to leave it? Is Frank walking heavy-footed around his den, and is he the one opening the doors to the cupboard where he once kept his finest Scotch whisky? And is his wife appearing in the hall, or clinking cups and saucers as she prepares to serve tea to some of her lady friends? Some people think so. But what about the lighter footsteps and the water taps and lights being turned on? Could another spirit — a young and mischievous one — also be lingering in the mansion?

A few people have felt particularly uneasy in some rooms in the basement where the Beban family's servants had lived. One of these servants, a Chinese boy, had died there, and a psychic researcher who visited the house strongly sensed his spirit's presence on that lower floor. Is it his ghost, with hair in a traditional Chinese braid, that appeared in the daycare children's artwork? Maybe, after so many lonely years in the empty house, the boy's spirit introduced itself to the children, hoping they would want to play with him and his red ball.

HALLOWEEN HORROR

Saint John, New Brunswick

There are those who believe that an unsettling air remains at the scene of a particularly vicious crime long after it is committed. That may explain why, for years after the murders of Maggie Vail and her baby girl, Ella May, horses would balk as they approached a certain spot on Black River Road in Saint John, New Brunswick.

In September of 1869, children out berry-picking discovered the skeletal remains of mother and child in a wooded area near the road. They couldn't be identified right away, but as news of the horrifying discovery spread, people came forward with clues that led authorities to identify the victims and, after two weeks, to charge a man named John A. Munroe with their murders.

The people of Saint John were shocked. John Munroe

was a pillar of the community. He was a well-known architect who had designed several buildings in the town. Though he had a wife and two young children, he had taken up with Maggie Vail — and little Ella May was his daughter. Munroe claimed he was innocent of the murders, but he was tried, found guilty and sentenced to death. The week before he was hanged in February of 1870, he finally confessed that he had killed Maggie and Ella on October 31 — All Hallow's Eve — in 1868.

John A. Munroe is buried in Fernhill Cemetery in Saint John. Over the years a story has persisted that on Halloween night an eerie green glow emanates from beneath his tombstone. It's said that teenagers dare one another to steal onto the property and check it out, but no one has spoken publicly about doing so. Were they too afraid to go? Or too afraid of what they saw? Whatever their reasons, they remain as silent as the grave.

The gravestone of John A. Munroe

BLOOD IN THE BARBERSHOP

Barkerville, British Columbia

A ghostly apparition played a part in another infamous case of murder — the fatal shooting of Charles Morgan Blessing in northern British Columbia in 1866.

Blessing, like so many other prospectors, was following the gold that had been luring thousands of people to the Pacific coast ever since the rush to California began in 1848. Blessing had left San Francisco for B.C.'s Cariboo Mountains in 1866, hoping for another chance to make his fortune. He was heading for Barkerville, a boom town that sprang up after Billy Barker struck it rich mining gold on nearby Williams Creek in 1862.

Along the way, Blessing met a travelling barber named Wellington Delaney Moses, and the two men journeyed on together. Later they were joined by a third man, James

Barry, whom Moses thought was a bit of a suspicious character. When the trio reached Quesnel, Moses decided to stay for a while. He could earn a little extra money there giving haircuts to men who stopped over in the town to pick up supplies. Since he and Blessing had become friends, he promised to look him up when he reached Barkerville.

When Moses finally arrived in Barkerville, he opened his own barbershop. Business was brisk, and Moses figured his new friend Blessing would have no trouble finding him in town. But he never arrived. After several weeks, though, James Barry did — alone. He told Moses that Blessing had hurt his foot and had decided he couldn't make it to Barkerville.

A view of Barkerville, 1868

Moses had a gut feeling Barry wasn't telling the truth. He became even more concerned about what had happened when a customer showed up at the shop wearing a gold nugget lapel pin. The nugget, shaped like a skull, was unusual, but Moses had seen one just like it a few months earlier — pinned to the jacket of Charles Blessing. Questioned by Moses about how he had got the pin, the customer said a dance hall girl in town had given it to him. Moses found the woman and learned that James Barry had given it to her soon after he had shown up in Barkerville.

This news fuelled Moses' suspicions about Blessing's fate, but not nearly as much as did a horrifying incident a few weeks later. The barber was in his shop waiting for customers when Blessing suddenly appeared, wanting a shave. His friend was a mess. He was dirty, his clothes were in tatters, and the gleam of life had gone from his eyes. Moses immediately prepared a hot towel and wrapped Blessing's face in it, then reached for his razor. When he turned back, he recoiled in horror. The towel covering Blessing's face was wet through with blood. Trembling, he reached for a corner of the cloth, but suddenly the chair was empty. Blessing was gone, and so were any doubts Moses might have had that something terrible had happened to him.

Moses travelled to nearby Richmond to tell a judge about his suspicions and, based on his evidence about the gold pin and the discovery of Blessing's body hidden in the bush along the trail, the judge ordered Barry arrested. Blessing had been shot in the head — and Barry owned a gun that could have caused that fatal wound, adding to the case that was built against him when he was tried for Blessing's murder. Judge Matthew Begbie, perhaps

British Columbia's most famous judge, heard the case, and in August of 1867, found Barry guilty and sentenced him to hang. Barry's trip to the gallows was the first public execution in the Cariboo district of British Columbia.

After Blessing's corpse was discovered, Moses arranged for its burial and, with the help of donations from his customers, paid for a headstone for the grave. But it was only when Barry was convicted that Moses finally felt he had done all he could to get justice for the man he had befriended along the gold rush trail. Surely now Blessing would truly rest in peace, and the terrifying spectre of his tormented spirit would never haunt Moses again.

Chief Justice Sir Matthew Begbie, ca. 1875

Spirits Past and Present

The ghosts of Barkerville's colourful past still walk the streets here, as living locals dressed in period costumes recreate the gold-rush era for visitors. The famed Judge Begbie holds court, miners dig for gold, a blacksmith works his forge, and a long-skirted schoolmarm greets rambunctious pupils. It's all in good fun, and it definitely makes history come alive for tourists.

But there are a few characters who appear in Barkerville who were never given parts in the re-enactment scripts. And if they ever lived in the town, they're not alive now. There's the mysterious fellow sporting a top hat and tails who suddenly appears briefly on the left side of the stage at the Theatre Royal. There's also the attractive blond woman wearing a white dress who has been known to startle male guests by materializing in their rooms at the St. George Hotel. And often, when everyone has gone home for the night at the museum housed in the former Barkerville Hotel, people have reported seeing a ghostly apparition of a woman looking out of a window upstairs.

No one seems to know who these restless spirits might be, but their presence adds new meaning to the "ghost town" label that's often given to settlements in the area that were abandoned when the gold ran out.

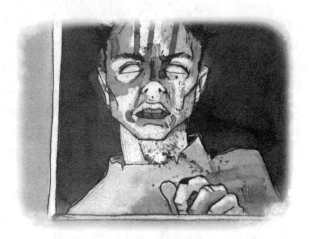

GHOSTLY BUSINESS

Halifax, Nova Scotia

In 1820 Alexander Keith, a young immigrant from Scotland, bought a brewery in Halifax and began a tradition of brewing fine beers in Nova Scotia. He had learned the business from an uncle in England a few years earlier, and used what he had learned to become a very successful businessman. He also became a prominent politician, actively involved in the development of Halifax and in the move to have Nova Scotia join Canada's Confederation in 1867. But he never stopped taking pride in his reputation as an excellent brewer.

Even now, he seems to linger, checking on the high standards he set nearly two centuries ago. Several workers at the Brewery Market on Halifax's Lower Water Street, home to Alexander Keith's Nova Scotia Brewery, are convinced it's his ghost that haunts the place. They've been startled when it makes its presence known in different parts of the establishment, but they're not too frightened by the sound of footsteps wandering through empty halls. They figure it's just Keith keeping an eye on what they're doing in his name.

However, there are a few very disturbing reports of *another* phantom lurking around the Brewery Market, and this one isn't friendly. It's the gory reflection of a blood-covered man that suddenly appears in a washroom mirror. When a terrified customer turns around to see what horror is behind him, he finds there's nothing there — and a hasty dash for the exit seems the best thing to do.

CREEPY CONFINEMENT

Ottawa, Ontario

Visitors looking for an inexpensive place to stay while touring Canada's capital often check into Ottawa's main youth hostel and, for some, the stay there is truly unforgettable.

The hostel is located at 72 Nicholas Street in a massive stone building that was home to the Carleton County Jail for more than a hundred years — from 1862 to 1972. Officially, only three hangings took place at the jail, but guards sometimes took it upon themselves to string up a prisoner from a beam near the gallows on the eighth floor, then cut down the body and watch it plummet to the courtyard below. Hundreds of other people died because of torturous treatment and miserable conditions in the jail. And thousands more — men, women and children —

died when, as newly arrived immigrants infected with scarlet fever, they were kept in the basement, in an attempt to control the spread of this highly contagious disease. The bodies of the infection-riddled victims were burned and their remains were buried on the grounds of the jail. Not surprising, then, are the many reports suggesting that the Ottawa Jail Hostel has some very creepy residents serving longer-than-life sentences.

Polly, an inmate at the Carleton County Jail, 1895

The most infamous criminal to be hanged at the jail was Patrick James Whelan. He was convicted of assassinating Thomas D'Arcy McGee, one of Canada's Fathers of Confederation. Whelan maintained his innocence right up to his death — an execution that was watched by a sensation-seeking crowd of five thousand. Since that fateful day in 1868, people have seen him walk toward the gallows many more times. His ghost has appeared in his cell on Death Row too, and even in the rooms of a few horrified guests.

Hostel visitors have also had nerve-racking encounters with other spirits that haunt the jail. They've been nudged in the back by an invisible presence, they've been startled by shadowy figures showing up at their doors, and they've been sent shivering from a location that is suddenly engulfed by icy blasts. They've heard chains rattling, pipes banging, cell doors clanging, children crying, women wailing, and men talking in empty rooms and hallways. And they've even had to listen to tales of a legendary evil vampire hiding out in the building — one rumoured to have feasted on the blood of children.

Despite such disturbing reports of otherworldly activity, the hostel continues to attract guests looking for reasonably priced rooms in an unusual setting rich in local history. Some even specifically check in hoping for a supernatural thrill. But folks who are easily frightened might want to think twice about staying there. The emotional price might be far too high for them to pay.

The courthouse and jail, ca. 1870-1880

DEADMAN'S ISLAND

Halifax, Nova Scotia

Elegant yachts now moor along the mainland side of Melville Island, a small island near the head of the Northwest Arm of Halifax Harbour in Nova Scotia. But in the early 1800s, this was a much grimmer place.

Back then, British navy warships dropped anchor there to unload French and American prisoners of war captured during the Napoleonic Wars and the War of 1812. The British had built a large military prison there in 1803 specifically to house such prisoners until they could be exchanged for their own captured soldiers and sailors. The captives were warned off trying to escape by being told, untruthfully, that the waters around the island were filled with hungry sharks.

But infectious diseases did claim the lives of some of

the men confined there in such close quarters. Their bodies were wrapped in shrouds and rowed to a nearby spit of land that prisoners called Target Hill — and that came to be known as Deadman's Island. Here the remains of close to two hundred American sailors and soldiers were buried in shallow graves. So were the bodies of one hundred black slaves who had abandoned the American army for the British and then succumbed to smallpox. Then came the Irish immigrants who had died of typhus fever.

Most of the prison buildings on Melville Island burned down in 1936, but over the years people would wander around Deadman's Island looking for relics of its past. And when they did, they occasionally discovered skeletal remains, giving rise to stories of ghosts haunting the old graveyard. Boys would challenge each other to sneak out to the end of the spit at night, and a few brave souls did spend some spine-tingling moments there, coming back with tales of spooky shapes moving around in the dark.

Some of those stories didn't seem so far-fetched, though, when workers became involved in preparations for building a development on Deadman's Island a few years ago. They felt uneasy when unusual lights began to appear among the trees they were planning to cut down. Glowing fires and mysterious lights have also been spotted by people looking across the harbour toward the island, and Alan Hatfield, a psychic visiting the site in 2002, heard the voices of three distinct male spirits.

In the late 1990s some Halifax residents started lobbying to have the spit of land preserved as a historic site, and they were eventually successful. Development plans were halted in 2000 when the city bought the property so it could be respectfully preserved as a burial ground. And in May of 2005, representatives of both the American and

Canadian armed forces took part in a ceremony marking the installation of a bronze plaque on a granite base to honour the memory of the Americans buried there.

At last, it seems, many restless souls have found peace. But strange lights are still occasionally spotted on Deadman's Island. And teenagers are still daring each other to head out that way after dark.

HEADLESS MARY

Montreal, Quebec

Most people don't go looking for ghosts, and most don't want ghosts to come looking for them. But for more than one hundred and thirty years, curiosity-seekers have gathered in Griffintown, an area of downtown Montreal near the Lachine Canal, hoping to see the ghost of a woman looking for her head. And over the years parents living in the area have warned their misbehaving young-sters that the headless ghost would come after them while she wandered around searching for it.

Griffintown was a bustling, working-class neighbour-hood of Montreal where thousands of Irish immigrants settled when they arrived in Canada in the nineteenth century. Life was hard for many of the people living there. It was certainly hard for two friends, Mary Gallagher and

Susan Kennedy, who were staying in a flat in a house at the corner of William and Murray Streets in the summer of 1879. On the night of June 27, they'd been socializing with a man named Michael Flanagan when they got into a terrible fight — and Mary Gallagher was killed. According to court documents, Susan Kennedy had knocked her to the floor and whacked her several times with an axe, chopping off her head. A neighbour living downstairs said the blows overhead were so violent that the ceiling plaster cracked, sending pieces showering down.

Susan Kennedy was found guilty of murdering her best friend. Her sentence — death by hanging — was supposed to be carried out on December 5, 1879, but a judge finally spared her life and sent her to prison instead. She was eventually paroled, after serving sixteen years in the Kingston Penitentiary in Ontario.

A Griffintown street during the spring floods, 1873

In the years following Mary Gallagher's death, several people reported seeing her on the streets of Griffintown, dressed as she had always been in life. And even though her ghost didn't always appear headless, people said she was looking for her head. As the number of Mary Gallagher sightings dwindled over time, locals began to talk about how she just appeared once every seven years — on the anniversary of her death.

Few traces of Gallagher's old neighbourhood remain in Montreal. Abandoned factories and slum housing have been replaced by film studios and trendy condos looking out over the Lachine Canal. But some folks still gather every seven years at the corner of William and Murray Streets to mark the passing of the lively, close-knit Irish-Canadian community that once was Griffintown. And they do so on June 27, just in case the headless ghost of Mary Gallagher decides to go for a walk that night.

A FINE HOME FOR A GHOST

Regina, Saskatchewan

It isn't only in Griffintown that people gather in the hopes of running into a ghost. Every October, groups of school-children have looked forward to class tours of Saskatchewan's Government House — because it's said to be haunted.

Government House is a splendid mansion located in Regina's Exhibition Park. Built in the early 1890s, it was at first home to the lieutenant-governor of the Northwest Territories, and then to the lieutenant-governor of Saskatchewan, after that province joined Confederation in 1905. In 1945, when World War II ended, the federal government moved the lieutenant-governor to the Hotel Saskatchewan and used the government residence to care for wounded veterans who had returned from combat.

Government House, ca. 1940s

Twelve years later, it became an adult education centre.

In the 1970s several groups interested in preserving Regina's historic sites organized an effort to restore the building to its original elegance, and in the 1980s it became Government House again. Lieutenant-governors didn't live in it anymore, but their offices have been there ever since, and it's where the Queen's representative hosts many special occasions. It's also home to a museum highlighting Saskatchewan's history.

The last lieutenant-governor to live in the mansion was Archibald McNab. He served the province in that position from 1936 to 1945. During that time a cook named Cheung became ill and died in his room in the servants' quarters. After his death people could still hear him shuffling around in his slippers through the house's many rooms. Some people still hear those footsteps.

The building's staff think it is Cheung's ghost that shifts things from one place to another, mysteriously opens and closes doors, flips up the corners of tablecloths, flushes toilets in empty bathrooms, and appears briefly in the kitchen every now and then. And even though it frightens some workers to feel an invisible presence hovering in the back stairwell, or to hear footsteps in the hall when they're alone, they've accepted the fact that a ghost has found a home in the mansion. They've even given him a nickname — Howie.

So Howie — whoever or whatever he is — gets blamed for all the strange goings-on in Government House. He's also the reason why youngsters are so willing to soak up a little history touring the stately home and museum. They're especially attracted by the program that runs in October. It's called "Halloween with Howie." It's fun, it's educational — and it sends shivers up their spines.

THE VOICE OF EVIL

Clarendon, Quebec

Susan Dagg liked her new log house. It was small — just one storey with an attic — but she, her husband, George, and their two young children, Susan and Johnny, were settling in nicely. They had built the home in 1889 on a farm at Clarendon, Quebec, a community on the Ottawa River about ten kilometres south of Shawville.

Imagine her disgust, then, when she returned from the cow barn after the morning milking to find her kitchen reeking of human feces. The filthy waste, most likely from the outhouse, had been smeared on the floor from one end of the house to the other. September 15, 1889, was turning out to be a very unpleasant day.

Two other children were living in the Dagg household at the time. One was Dinah Burden McLean, a poor eleven-year-old girl who had been sent from Scotland to an orphanage in Belleville — until a Canadian family came forward to give her a good home. The Daggs had adopted her with that in mind, and also in the hope that Dinah would help Mrs. Dagg care for the two younger children. The other was a second orphan, a boy named Dean who worked for various farmers in the area when they needed extra help.

Early on the morning of the 15th, Dean had found a five-dollar bill on the kitchen floor when he climbed down the ladder from his sleeping corner in the attic. In 1889, five dollars was a lot of money, and he had given the bill to Mr. Dagg, telling him where he had found it.

But George was suspicious. The night before, his wife had tucked that bill safely away in her dresser along with a two-dollar bill. After Dean headed outside to do some chores, George asked Susan to check the drawer to see if the two-dollar bill was still there. It wasn't. So George climbed up to the attic to look for it, and found it in Dean's bed.

Assuming that Dean was a thief, and that he had made the mess in the kitchen to distract them from the theft, the Daggs ordered him to leave and reported him to the local authorities. The next day, though, they weren't so sure they had done the right thing. Dean was gone, but the disgusting waste was back — in the cupboards, on the beds, and mixed in with the food supplies — and they had no clue who the nasty, filth-spreading culprit was. They had no idea, either, about who spilled milk, broke dishes, moved chairs, knocked over a table, and even splashed water in Mrs. Dagg's face.

Not only were the Daggs mystified about what was going on in their house — they were frightened. So when

George had to be away from home a few days later, he asked his father to come and stay at the house. That's how John Dagg ended up witnessing some of the spooky incidents plaguing his son's family. He was there when the windows started breaking. He went outside to try to catch the vandal but there was no one in sight.

To add to their misery, over the next several days the family had to put out dozens of small fires that broke out spontaneously — and one afternoon an invisible hand hacked off Dinah's long braid and cut out large chunks of young Johnny's hair. Then, just when the Daggs thought the situation couldn't get any worse, it did. The unseen force that had been tormenting them so terribly started targeting Dinah specifically. She began seeing a dark shape in the house when no one else could, and hearing a deep gravelly voice uttering shockingly crude and vulgar things. She was terrified, and so were the Daggs. Desperate for some peace, they sent Dinah to stay with John Dagg for a few days, and the haunting ceased. But as soon as Dinah returned, it resumed.

By then, word about what was happening at the Clarendon farm had spread throughout the district, and curious neighbours were showing up, hoping to see for themselves some of the eerie incidents. Desperate for an explanation, the Daggs consulted a fortune teller, brought in clergymen, and agreed to have a man named Percy Woodcock from Brockville, Ontario, spend some time with them investigating their plight.

Woodcock was a well-respected Canadian artist who was also very interested in paranormal, or supernatural, occurrences. Articles about the Clarendon spookiness in local Ottawa Valley newspapers had sparked his desire to learn more about it. He arrived at the Dagg farm on

November 16 and spent two days interviewing all family members and anyone else who had direct knowledge of the bizarre goings-on. He went outside with Dinah to a small shed where she had last seen the evil spirit that spoke to — and through — her. There he suffered through a stream of foul language and insults directed at him personally, including threats to break his neck if he didn't leave.

More encounters with the snarling, invisible speaker continued the next afternoon — when a crowd of neighbours gathered to watch Woodcock challenge the phantom to identify itself. In turn, it claimed to be both a devil and an angel, leaving observers frightened and confused. After Woodcock left, a minister arrived and the crowd started singing hymns. The ghoulish spirit joined in briefly, laughing at efforts to drive it away, and then it left, threatening to return the next day.

Woodcock kept detailed notes of everything that had happened at the Dagg farm in the fall of 1889. He also obtained signed statements from several other witnesses, and published his findings in a long report in a Brockville newspaper. He made no mention of the torment continuing after November 19, and there is no known record that it did. Why it ended suddenly after an agonizing two months, or why it began in the first place, has never been explained.

Some locals at the time thought the whole affair was a hoax. But why would the Daggs and Dinah try to fool people in such a way? What could they hope to gain, other than a lot of negative publicity? Besides, Woodcock made it very clear that he believed the Daggs and Dinah were sincere and truthful as well as confused and terrified.

There were some suggestions that a poltergeist might

have been responsible for the bizarre events at Clarendon. A poltergeist is said to be a mischievous, sometimes mean, spirit that does things like make strange noises, shake and rattle furniture and windows, snatch and grab small items, and send things flying around a room. It's usually active at night, and most often makes its presence known in a household that includes a teenaged girl who's under some emotional strain. After a few days or weeks, it seems to stop what it's doing as suddenly as it started.

A poltergeist haunting might very well explain what happened to the Daggs and Dinah. Maybe Dinah deeply missed her home in Scotland, leaving her vulnerable to an encounter with a nasty spirit such as this one. But there's no record of a poltergeist ever speaking through a person the way the Clarendon ghost did, and the identity of the evil presence that possessed Dinah — and haunted her new home in Canada — remains a mystery to this day.

GÎRL ÎN THE RÎVER

Pain Court, Ontario

Pain Court is a village located on the Thames River near Chatham, Ontario. It was settled in the late 1700s by poor immigrants from the Detroit area of Michigan who moved onto Native lands here. By the 1820s it had become one of the earliest French-speaking communities in southern Ontario. The village's historical significance is highlighted on a plaque put up by the Ontario Heritage Foundation in front of Pain Court's Church of the Immaculate Conception. What the plaque doesn't say is that the area is reported to have been haunted for the last hundred or so years by a ghost.

It's thought that this restless soul is the spirit of Mary Jacobs, a young woman who had fallen for a man named Alex Miller. Her parents weren't impressed with this young fellow; in fact, they were furious that their daughter was seeing him. But Mary was in love with Alex and, according to her parents, after a big argument with them, she ran off with him. Some days later, she turned up dead.

According to one version of the story, Mary's putrid body was found partially buried behind the barn on the family farm, showing signs of death by foul play. Another story claims it was first hidden on the property and then thrown into the Thames, where it was found floating downstream. Even though the body bore marks of a severe beating, local authorities decided Mary had committed suicide by drowning herself.

Publicly, Mary's parents blamed Alex for her death, but privately they knew that he'd had nothing to do with it. Apparently, during the fight with their daughter over her choice of boyfriend, Mrs. Jacobs had flown into a rage and had beaten her daughter to death with a heavy iron. Then the couple had tried to cover up the crime — and since Mary's death was ruled a suicide, it looks as if, officially, they succeeded.

Over the years, the phantom presence of a young woman has been seen at different places along the river near the spot where Mary's body was found. There was even one report years ago of a young minister, a Reverend Knight, being scared out of his wits when he saw a woman's body floating in the river, only to have the vision suddenly disappear. Some local residents say it's Mary who haunts the Thames around Pain Court, looking for the young man she fell in love with. But maybe her spirit can't find peace because of the terrible way she died — at the hands of her own mother.

THE PHANTOM STEAMSHIP

Lake Superior, Ontario

For at least two hundred years, sailors worldwide have shared tales of seeing a ship called the *Flying Dutchman* — but they haven't all been talking about the same vessel. The original *Flying Dutchman* was probably a ship captained by a Dutchman named Hendrik van der Decken more than three hundred and fifty years ago. The ship never made it back to its home port of Amsterdam, Holland, and it was generally believed that it sank during a storm in the dangerous waters around the Cape of Good Hope at the southern tip of Africa.

But time and again, long after van der Decken's ship was lost, captains of other sailing ships reported seeing the doomed vessel and its ghostly crew. In some cases they even got close enough to the Dutchman's ship to hear him ask them to take some letters home. It was rumoured that any ship agreeing to take those letters from van der Decken would also be swallowed up by stormy seas. And so the legend of the *Flying Dutchman* was born, and lives on to this day.

Over time the "Flying Dutchman" tag came to mean any ghost ship fated to sail for all eternity the waters where it sank, and many different Flying Dutchmen are said to sail the world's seas and oceans. The mysterious fate of the steamship *Bannockburn* has earned it the spooky reputation of being the *Flying Dutchman* of Canada's largest, coldest and deepest Great Lake — Lake Superior.

The *Bannockburn* was a sturdy, all-steel steamer built in England in 1893 for the Montreal Transportation Company. At 74.7 metres, it was designed specifically to be just under the length restriction at the time for ships navigating the Great Lakes waterway. Any longer and they couldn't fit easily in the locks of the Welland Canal, which connects Lake Ontario and Lake Erie.

On November 20, 1902, the *Bannockburn* finished taking on a full load of wheat at Port Arthur, Ontario (now Thunder Bay). It was to deliver the wheat to the port at Midland, Ontario, on Lake Huron's Georgian Bay. Early the next morning it left Port Arthur and made for the open waters of Lake Superior. By late afternoon, despite a strong headwind, it was already nearly one hundred kilometres southeast of Passage Island. James McMaugh, captain of the *Algonquin*, a steamer sailing toward Port Arthur, spotted the *Bannockburn* and kept an eye on its progress for several minutes. At one point, though, he turned away briefly to deal with something that required his attention. When he looked back a minute or two later, he was surprised to find that he could no longer see the *Bannockburn*. It was as if it had suddenly disappeared.

Assuming the steamer had been hidden behind a distant bank of fog, McMaugh sailed on, not worrying about what had happened until he heard later that the *Bannockburn* hadn't stopped in at Sault Ste. Marie as planned. In fact, after McMaugh's sighting, the *Bannockburn* was never seen again.

The waters of Lake Superior can be dangerous. Powerful storms often build up without warning, especially in the cold, wind-plagued month of November. After days of searching without success for the *Bannockburn*, everyone concluded that a deadly Lake Superior storm had claimed yet another ship and twenty-two more victims — the crew aboard the *Bannockburn*.

But starting in 1903, sailors on watch duty began to report seeing the *Bannockburn*, its running lights still working, churning through choppy waters toward Sault Ste. Marie. Other reports described the ship as being covered with ice, a ghostly white apparition sailing off into the darkness. And a few seamen even spoke in hushed tones of how they had seen skeleton-like crewmen with hollow eyes manning the ghost ship as it sailed silently by.

The Bannockburn downbound on the St. Mary's River between Lake Superior and Lake Huron in the summer of 1902

What happened to the *Bannockburn* — why it sank without warning, and where — is still a mystery. But it's not hard to see why the steamer has come to be known as the *Flying Dutchman* of Lake Superior, doomed to sail that Great Lake's waters for all eternity.

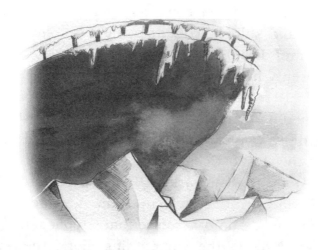

THE SHIP THAT WOULDN'T DIE

Arctic Ocean

Another sturdy steel cargo steamer, the *Baychimo*, also came to be known as a ghost ship, but not because it sank without a trace with all hands on board, only to reappear months or years later. In a way, the *Baychimo*'s fate was the exact opposite of the *Bannockburn*'s in that it seemed to be unsinkable, and ended up being dubbed "the ship that wouldn't die."

In 1969 a group of Inuit hunters reported seeing the *Baychimo* adrift in the Chukchi Sea, just west of Point Barrow, the northernmost tip of Alaska. Until then, everyone who knew about the cargo ship had assumed it had finally sunk. After all, the last time anyone had seen it was seven years before, in 1962, when some Inuit kayakers spotted it in the icy waters of the Beaufort Sea.

But people's assumptions about the fate of the *Baychimo* had been proven wrong before, so the fact that it was seen again didn't come as such a great surprise. What was, and still is, truly amazing is the fact that the *Baychimo* first disappeared way back in 1931.

The seventy-metre-long cargo ship had been built in Sweden in 1914. In 1919 the Hudson's Bay Company bought it and had it refitted. It had to be able to withstand the hazards it would encounter sailing the treacherous waters of the Arctic Ocean. In 1921 it was sent to the eastern Arctic to visit various HBC outposts on Baffin Island — where Inuit hunters came to trade furs in exchange for food and other essential supplies. In 1925 it was assigned to do the same thing along the western Arctic's shores.

In early July of 1931, with Captain John Cornwell at the helm and a crew of thirty-six on board, the *Baychimo* set sail from Vancouver on its regular annual trading run up the west coast of British Columbia, around Alaska, and through the Beaufort Sea to Victoria Island in the Arctic. But this trip would prove to be anything but regular. The outward-bound portion of the journey was going well, and the *Baychimo*'s hold was carrying nearly a full load of furs and skins when Captain Cornwall decided to cut short the trip after reaching Coppermine (now Kugluktuk) on September 5. He was worried because he was encountering more large ice floes than he expected to see at that time of the year. His fears were not unfounded. Disaster struck on the return voyage. That September winter came early to the Arctic, and on October 9, the ship found itself trapped in ice about one and a half kilometres from shore near Barrow, Alaska.

Via the ship's radio, Captain Cornwall arranged for

planes to pick up half the men as soon as weather permitted. Then he and sixteen remaining crew members began preparations to spend the winter with the steamer and its valuable cargo. The plan was to build a hut on shore, stocking it with supplies they hauled over the ice from the ship. They were also to store on shore as many of the fur bales as they could manage to move. And everything went according to plan at first.

All of the crew had moved into the large shack by the end of October and they were getting by fairly well, despite crowded conditions and the depressing lack of daylight at that time of year. The shack was actually warmer than the ship. But on November 24 gale-force winds and blinding snow began battering the shelter, and the men were forced to stay indoors for two days. On the morning of the 26th, when the storm had died down a little, they emerged from the hut to be greeted by an amazing sight. Snow and ice piled nearly six metres high had built up where the *Baychimo* had been trapped, and the ship was nowhere to be seen. Had the steamer been pushed underwater by that massive mountain of ice and snow? That's what most of the men thought, and the captain radioed HBC headquarters with the bad news.

But on December 3, Captain Cornwall received a message that shocked everyone. The *Baychimo* had been sighted about eighty kilometres north of their location, trapped in ice about eight kilometres off shore. A small group of Inuit and white trappers made several trips to the ship, taking away most things of value, including the remaining bales of furs. Those men reported that the steamer had a hole in its side, and would most likely sink as soon as the ice broke up.

Clearly then there was no longer any reason for

Captain Cornwall and his crew to spend the winter in their makeshift accommodations, and planes were finally able to reach them during the second week of February of 1932. They were all greatly relieved that the last voyage of the *Baychimo* had finally come to an end, with everyone returning home safely.

But while the voyage may have ended for the crew, it was far from over for their ship. It was almost as if, once freed from the control of human hands, the *Baychimo* had taken on a life of its own. Against all odds, it survived the next thaw, and many others afterward, and continued to sail the waters of the western Arctic. It was seen three times over the next two years, and again in 1935 and 1939. After World War II, researchers and explorers joined Inuit kayakers and dogsledders in reporting they had seen "the ship that wouldn't die." Looking ever more rusty and battered as time passed, it still managed to survive decades of brutal Arctic winters and to continue on its

The Baychimo *lies high and dry on ice, 2.4 km from Barrow, Alaska, 1933.*

mysterious voyage to some unknown destination, dodging deadly icebergs along the way.

It's been nearly forty years since the Inuit hunters reported seeing the *Baychimo* afloat back in 1969. Surely it must have sunk by now. But who knows? People have believed that many times before, and over and over the sturdy steel steamer proved them wrong. Maybe it really is a ship that will never die.

THE INVISIBLE BEAST

Moser River, Nova Scotia

Moser River is a small village on Nova Scotia's coastal Highway 7, just west of the Halifax-Guysborough county line. The village takes its name from the river on which it was built, and both were named after Henry Moser. He bought land and settled in the area in the late 1700s.

Life in Moser River during the first half of the twentieth century was still pretty much as quiet and slow-paced as it had been for Moser's children and grandchildren. People made a living fishing, farming and working in the lumber business. Spending time with neighbours singing, playing the fiddle, step-dancing or playing cards was a pleasant break from the demands of work and daily chores.

Back in the early 1900s Bob Lowe, a Moser River resi-dent, had just spent an enjoyable evening like that the night he got the fright of his life. It was raining when he left his neighbour's house, so he pulled up his coat collar and set out along the road toward home. Suddenly, out of nowhere, he heard a scrambling noise in the bushes. Then something unseen rammed into him, pulling off his coat and knocking him down as it raced past.

Lowe picked himself up, reached down for his muddy coat and, after a quick look around, ran home as fast as his trembling legs could take him. But even though he was scared, he was also curious about what had happened, so when he calmed down he went back out to the road armed with a rifle and a lantern. When he reached the spot where he had been attacked, he carefully examined the muddy ground and nearby bushes along the roadside. But try as he might, he couldn't find a single trace of who or what had struck him. All he could see were his own footprints. Then he heard the noise again.

This time Lowe could make out the sounds of a four-footed creature moving quickly toward him, but once again he could see nothing. He shouted into the darkness, hoping to scare off the invisible beast, but it kept coming. Once again Lowe started running as fast as he could. The phantom pursued him relentlessly until he neared home. Then its sounds suddenly faded into the darkness, leaving behind no evidence at all of its horrifying presence. But traces of the spooky run-in on the road near Moser River would remain burned in Lowe's memory until the day he died.

THE GHOSTS OF WAR

Fort Erie, Ontario

Each summer crowds of visitors take in the sights and sounds of battle re-enactments at the "Old Fort" in Fort Erie, Ontario. And every now and then a few of them have an unsettling encounter with a ghost from the distant past.

On the Lake Erie shore near the international Peace Bridge to Buffalo, New York, the fort played an important role in the War of 1812. The British army first built a small fort there in 1764 and used it to stockpile supplies during the American Revolution in the late 1770s and early 1780s. But in 1799 surging, ice-congested water flowed out of the lake into the Niagara River and washed most of the structure away. The same thing happened to its replacement in 1803, and the third, new-and-improved fort wasn't yet finished when the war between the Americans and the British, including Britain's Canadian colonies, began in 1812.

Troops stationed at Fort Erie at the time left it unfinished, taking supplies and weapons with them. The Americans took it over for a while in 1813, but abandoned it by the end of the year, when the British returned and resumed construction. The Americans captured it in July of 1814, and held off a major British attack that left more than one thousand British and Canadian soldiers dead. The British then laid siege to the fort and the Americans finally abandoned it for good in November of 1814, destroying much of it before leaving.

The Niagara Parks Commission restored Fort Erie in the late 1930s. During reconstruction, the remains of one hundred and fifty British and three American soldiers were found, and a monument was erected to mark their mass grave. Every August pretend "soldiers" stage the 1814 siege during which some of those men may have died. But could it be that the spirits of a few of the fort's former inhabitants may be taking their places among the actors?

One mysterious, uniformed soldier has appeared in the dining hall when no re-enactments were being staged, and another has been spotted hovering in a darkened corner of the fort. The bedding on an old bunk on display in the fort is often found rumpled and tossed as if someone has been sleeping there, and a shadowy woman — perhaps the ghost of an officer's wife — occasionally appears briefly in the sleeping quarters.

The lingering spirits of any number of individuals who died violently at the fort might account for such ghostly presences at the historic site, but it's the blood-chilling appearances of two specific soldiers that seem to have the strongest connections to Fort Erie's past. Some archaeological evidence appears to back up old journal entries referring to what happened to these two unfortunate souls.

Back in the summer of 1814 an American sergeant named Benjamin White was getting a shave from another soldier when the room that the two men were in was hit by British cannon fire. White was decapitated and the barber's hands were blown off. Surely this story explains the scariest ghosts of all that haunt the for — a soldier with no hands and one with no head.

Soldiers guard the inner gate at the entrance to Old Fort Erie.

GALLOPING GHOSTS

Bad Hills, Saskatchewan

Several years ago George Redhead, a farmer near Bickleigh in the Bad Hills region of Saskatchewan, had settled down for the night after a long day of plowing. He had camped out beside his truck so he'd be ready to get back to work as soon as the sun came up. Just as he was about to doze off, he heard the sound of a horse galloping toward him. He wondered who might be riding out there after dark, but didn't think too much about it until he realized that the hoof beats were getting louder and closer by the second.

Redhead began to panic. What if the rider didn't see his little campsite in the dark and rode right over him? He jumped up and moved forward, intending to wave off the unexpected visitor. But as his eyes adjusted to the moonlight, he was amazed to find there was no rider — and no horse — anywhere in sight. And yet the invisible horse kept coming until it swept past him and away, back into the still silence of the night. Dazed and bewildered, Redhead tried to settle back down, but sleep didn't come easily that night.

Years earlier, in 1932, two sisters from Bickleigh had a much quieter encounter with a ghostly galloper. At least they could see the wispy apparition that pounded toward them. But unlike George Redhead, Annie and Ivy Bristow couldn't hear a sound as the creature approached. In fact, it was the silence that frightened them most.

The Bristow sisters had been riding home in their horse-drawn sleigh when they noticed the phantom horse and rider loping along the train tracks. As the two women approached the point where the tracks crossed the road, their horses suddenly dug in, refusing to pull the sleigh any further until the spooky vision had passed. Only after it had raced off into the darkness did the sisters' team move. Then the two horses dashed off without waiting for a command, only slowing to a trot when they and the terrified travellers had reached the safety of the Bristows' lane.

In the 1850s and '60s, Metis from the White Horse Plains galloped across the Bad Hills, hunting buffalo. After Henry Wason, Bickleigh's first pioneer, settled in the area, other immigrants followed — riding horses to hunt, clear the land and visit neighbouring homesteads. Soldiers, fur traders, mail carriers, travelling preachers and schoolchildren also rode horses in and around Bickleigh well into the twentieth century. Was the ghostly rider the spirit of one of them? No one knows.

THE LADY IN RED

Toronto, Ontario

Toronto's subway system has two Bay Street stations — the one thousands of riders walk through every day, and another one below it that is closed to the public. Lower Bay, as it's known, was opened back in 1966 to help link the new east-west Bloor-Danforth to the existing north-south Yonge Street line. But after just six months, the Toronto Transit Commission decided it was better to keep the two lines separate, because when a train broke down on either line the entire system ground to a halt. So the stairs connecting the upper and lower Bay stations were blocked off, and the white-tiled lower station became a storage site for escalator parts and some maintenance equipment.

These days Lower Bay is often used by television and

film crews shooting subway scenes. It's still used for storage too, and for testing new system signs and experimenting with possible changes to subway platforms. But a few TTC employees don't like being asked to spend time down there, especially not at night, because they don't want to meet up with the station's ghost.

The spectral "lady in red" drifts through the tunnel toward the station, occasionally moaning pitifully as she approaches. Wavy brown hair frames her face and falls across the shoulders of her long red dress. The apparition lasts just twenty to thirty seconds, but that's more than enough time for a frightened observer to see the dark hollows where her eyes should be. Even more disturbing is how she moves. She seems to have no legs — appearing to float just above the ground.

Is this lady in red the ghost of a victim of some terrible crime on the station platform, or of a tragic accident on the tracks below? No one knows. But it's easy to understand why a worker seeing her late at night wouldn't look forward to the possibility of encountering her ever again.

SPIRIT WALK

Toronto, Ontario

During the 1990s another Toronto location was a very popular choice for film and television producers, especially those who were trying to recreate scenes from the nineteenth century.

The area known as the Distillery District lies near Lake Ontario just east of Toronto's downtown core. It features some of the finest examples of brick and stone industrial buildings erected in the early to mid-1800s, and has been designated a national historic site. In the early 2000s, major restoration and renovations transformed the property into a contained, no-cars-allowed, village-like setting for boutiques, cafés, restaurants and art galleries. The new and improved Distillery District welcomed the public in 2003.

However, when it was used as a film set — and during its most recent transformation — ghostly goings-on at this place left some people feeling a little uncomfortable. Items moved mysteriously from one place to another, doors opened and shut on their own and strange sounds echoed from vacant nooks and crannies. One member of a television crew even reported seeing the spectre of a middle-aged man pass right through a closed door.

But some people say such unnerving incidents are nothing new, and that rumours of the Distillery District being haunted date much further back — to 1834. That was two years after James Worts, the original owner, built the first mill to grind grain on the site. Worts emigrated from England in 1831. The next year his brother-in-law, William Gooderham, joined him in Toronto and became his business partner. In time Worts's eldest son and Gooderham would go on to expand the milling business and build a distillery to process grain into whisky.

A view of The Distillery District

Unfortunately, Worts himself never lived to see the Gooderham and Worts Distillery Company become one of the most successful businesses in Toronto's history. In 1834 his world was shattered when his beloved wife died during childbirth. Twelve days later his body was found in a deep well on the property. No one knows for sure, but talk at the time suggested he was so depressed after his wife's death that he deliberately threw himself into the well. But whether it was suicide or an accident, Worts's tragic end seems to have marked the beginning of a series of eerie occurrences, leading to the belief that the Distillery District buildings are haunted by the ghost of James Worts himself.

But why would his ghost wander around the place? Does he have some unfinished business to attend to where he built the mill so long ago? Or is he still lingering near where he died, hoping to connect to the spirit of his beloved wife — so they can be reunited in death?

FRÎGHT NÎGHT

Victoria, British Columbia

The two Australian women camped out in the sprawling gardens of a vacant old mansion in Victoria in the early 1960s felt quite comfortable as they settled down for the night. They were experienced world travellers who didn't take foolish risks, and they had chosen their campsite with safety in mind. It couldn't be seen from the street and nobody else was hanging around the place. Besides, the price was right — it was free — and the view from the back end of the property — a rippling, moonlit tidal inlet known as the Gorge Waterway — was breathtaking. So they were totally unprepared for what happened a few hours after they fell asleep.

The shouting woke them both at the same time. Startled, they looked around. In the shadows they thought they could make out the dark figure of a small woman who kept shrieking at them to get out. They jumped up and started packing up their kits, anxious to move on. But suddenly the shouting stopped and they were alone again. Feeling confused and a little foolish, they took a few deep breaths to calm down, and then decided to stay where they were and try to get some more sleep. But neither of them got any more rest that night.

As soon as they slipped back into their sleeping bags the women were overcome by a sense of some invisible presence — a presence seething with hate because they were still there. They were exhausted and didn't want to move if they didn't have to, but the feeling of resentment became so unbearable that they finally packed up their belongings and nervously waited for dawn on the nearby bridge across the gorge. And as if they hadn't already been frightened enough that night, while sitting on the bridge their eyes became riveted on a mysterious red light that hovered in mid-air, moving back and forth just above the water below.

When a woman named Inez O'Reilly heard about the Australians' harrowing experience a few years later, she wasn't the least bit surprised. Learning where it had happened, she had no doubt that the women had had a run-in with her husband's grandmother, Caroline O'Reilly. Caroline would never have approved of the female travellers' unladylike behaviour. Ladies in her day wouldn't have dressed casually and would never have camped out on their own under the stars.

But Caroline's day was long gone. Nearly a hundred years earlier, in 1867, she and her husband, Peter O'Reilly, had moved into their new home on Pleasant Street, a fifteen-room mansion known as Point Ellice House. The garden of that house was the very place the

Australian women had chosen for their campsite. By then, Caroline had been dead for more than sixty years.

Inez O'Reilly and her husband John moved into Point Ellice House soon after they married in 1965, and almost immediately Inez felt Caroline's presence in the place. The mansion had been neglected for a long time, and Inez and John felt compelled to restore it to its original grandeur. After two years of expensive and time-consuming effort, they opened Point Ellice House to the public.

But some visitors got to see more than the beautifully restored rooms and furnishings. They got to see Grandmother Caroline too. One child touring the house with her own grandmother left screaming because of her ghostly presence. Some people felt an invisible hand tap them on the shoulder. And one group on tour apparently spent nearly an hour with Caroline's daughter, Kathleen.

That happened on a day when Inez was so busy outdoors that she forgot about the group waiting to be shown around. When she finally realized her mistake she rushed back into the house, embarrassed and eager to apologize. But to her surprise, the visitors were preparing to leave, saying that the nice young woman in a blue dress had done a lovely job of conducting the tour.

Inez was stunned. Other than the tourists, she was the only one at the house that day. Curious, she took a few members of the group upstairs to Kathleen's room and pointed out a blue dress on display there. She asked if any of them recognized it. They all said they did, insisting that it was just like the one worn by the young woman who had given them the tour. Inez was convinced then that the ghost of her husband's Aunt Kathleen, who had lived in the house until her death in 1945, must have been the woman who ushered the guests through the place.

There have been other reports of appearances by Kathleen outside the house near the garden gate. Some people also believe that the ghost of Kathleen's brother, Frank, makes his presence known every now and then, speaking in a loud voice in what was once his bedroom. But Inez O'Reilly believed that because of the way she acted, it was Caroline, and no one else, who drove the Australian women from her garden more than forty years ago.

As for the mysterious red light that the two women saw hovering over the gorge, several people think they have an explanation for that eerie experience too. On May 26, 1896, the original bridge spanning the gorge collapsed, sending dozens of people aboard a tramcar plunging to a horrible death. The bodies of fifty-five men, women and children were recovered, but it was assumed that the death toll was even higher. Those who have seen the red light hovering above the water say it's the glow of a lantern carried by a spirit still looking for a loved one lost in the collapse.

Obviously, the Australians had no idea when they rolled out their sleeping bags that their chosen campsite was rumoured to be one of the most haunted locations in Victoria. If they had, that was the last place they would have chosen to spend their first night in the city, even if the price was right and the view breathtaking.

NOTES FROM NOWHERE

Winnipeg, Manitoba

Churches are seen as places of refuge, offering peace and comfort to all who enter. But the sudden arrival of a mysterious presence in a church can disturb its peace and trouble the souls of those present. Such an event took place at St. John's Anglican Cathedral in Winnipeg more than fifty years ago.

The cathedral stands across the street from St. John's Park, near the Redwood Avenue Bridge spanning the Red River. In 1817 Lord Selkirk set aside the land on which it is built for a church and a school to be used by the area's first European settlers, the Red River colonists. In 1822 a small mission church was constructed on part of what is now the cemetery. In 1833 a new, larger church was built where the current cathedral now stands, and a third one was erected in 1862. The existing church was built in 1926, using much of the stone from the previous two structures.

In 1927 a classic Casavant pipe organ was installed in the new church. Thirty-six years later that fine musical instrument would be the source of a very mysterious disturbance in the history-rich house of worship.

In December of 1953, a small group of parishioners gathered in the cathedral's chapel one Sunday afternoon to reflect on the meaning of Advent, a time when Christians prepare spiritually for the coming of Christmas. Reverend John Ogle Anderson, the rector or senior clergyman, was there, as was his assistant, a curate named Reverend H. J. Skynner.

Reverend Skynner had planned a very simple, informal service of scripture readings and prayer. But as he began his first reading, any plans for simplicity went right out the stained glass windows. Suddenly a single, flute-sounding organ note echoed through the building. Then another note. And another. No harmony was added, just single notes played slowly, one by one, with the flute stop pulled out.

The dozen or so parishioners present that afternoon were surprised to hear the strange melody interrupt the rector's reading. The organist wasn't known for making mistakes like that. But the rector and the dean were even more astonished. The organist wasn't there. And from where he was sitting in the chapel, Reverend Anderson could see that no one else was sitting in front of the instrument's two-tiered keyboard.

The haunting sounds continued to resonate throughout the cathedral for several minutes that afternoon. The next day the rector called in the technician who regularly serviced the organ, but the man could see nothing wrong with it. What's more, he found that all the stops, including the flute stop, were pushed in, preventing any wind from entering the pipes to make a sound. The organ had not been touched after the disturbingly strange episode and, set like that, it shouldn't have been able to make any sound at all. So the technician couldn't come up with any earthly explanation. Neither could the rector or the curate, and the identity of the invisible organ player with the ghostly tune remains a mystery to this day.

A HAUNTING MELODY

Edmonton, Alberta

A legend about another invisible organ player persists at the University of Alberta in Edmonton, but this phantom musician didn't play only one note, and didn't just play one time either.

Its instrument of choice was the War Memorial Organ installed after World War I in the university's original Convocation Hall. To honour individuals from the university who lost their lives during both the First and Second World Wars, their names are listed on plaques at the hall's entrance.

Perhaps the invisible organist also wanted to honour the war dead. It's rumoured that night after night, during World War II, the organ played "Taps" — the haunting twenty-four-note melody heard at American military funerals and memorial services and at informal Canadian services too. But there was no one to be seen anywhere near the keyboard when it did.

The pipes of the War Memorial Organ, 1941

A SPiRiTED PERFORMANCE

Uptergrove, Ontario

By contrast, the ghostly organist at St. Columbkille's Church at Uptergrove, near Orillia, had no problem with being visible. He was even dressed for the occasion when he gave a brief recital in late March of 1964. More than forty years later, Susan Wallace could still clearly remember how he looked and how upset she was when she saw him.

Wallace and her two sisters were helping their mother and another woman clean the church just before Easter. Suddenly a mysterious, white-faced figure — all dressed in black and wearing a top hat — appeared in the choir loft. He sat down at the organ and began to play.

Worried that the stranger might be up to no good, her mother and the other woman climbed the stairs to ask him what he was doing there. When they reached the loft, he backed away without answering and entered the bell tower room, letting the door to it swing closed after him. The two women followed him, but were completely taken aback to find that the small, windowless room was empty. The door they had just come through was the only way in and out of the room, and the white-faced man hadn't gone past them. He had simply disappeared.

DINING WITH THE DEAD

Vancouver, British Columbia

Old buildings sometimes have strange tales to tell. The Century Inn and Bar, which opened in 2006, is an elegant restaurant on Richards Street near Pender Avenue in downtown Vancouver. It's located in Century House, a classic heritage building constructed in 1911 as a Canada Permanent Mortgage bank. After the bank closed in 1951, several other businesses set up shop there, including an insurance company, a trade school, a bookstore and another fine restaurant.

Sean Sherwood, the owner of the latest restaurant, personally supervised the restoration and remodelling of the building, but there were times when he felt some other-worldly spirit was also keeping a ghostly eye on what was happening. Occasionally when he was the only one in the place, he would hear mysterious laughter and haunting footsteps. He also got cell phone calls from what he believed was a female ghost.

What's more, a carpenter reported seeing a strange woman in old-fashioned clothes walking around the place. When he asked her to leave, she gave him such a scary look that he left instead, and wouldn't work in the building alone after that. Other workers also sensed the ghostly presence of a woman, and since the restaurant opened, some servers and diners have been disturbed by the sounds of a woman crying in an empty washroom stall.

Sherwood was aware of rumours that Century House was haunted when he finalized plans to open his new restaurant there. He'd heard the tale of how, decades ago, a female clerk was shot at the bank — either during a robbery or by her enraged husband. No one seems to have verified this story, but if it's true, could it be that the murdered woman's spirit is the otherworldly presence lingering in Century House?

THE PHANTOM TRAIN

Medicine Hat, Alberta

In 1908 Bob Twohey was working as a railway engineer on the Canadian Pacific Railway line in Alberta. He had a wife and children to support in Medicine Hat. One night in May he was in the cab of a train rolling along just south of there when a blinding light suddenly appeared in front of him. The closer it came, the more terrified Twohey became. Realizing that another locomotive was speeding toward him, he was about to shout to Gus Day, the fire-man working with him, to jump. But at that moment the collision-bound train, its whistle blaring, swerved to the right and raced past his train into the darkness, its pas-sengers waving from the windows.

Twohey had no idea what had just happened. A train couldn't possibly have passed his. There was just one track on that part of the line and his engine and cars were still on it. Figuring his imagination must have been playing tricks on him, he decided to say nothing to Day. However, he was troubled enough by the frightening experience that he asked to be allowed to do work around the railway yards for a while. It wasn't until a couple of weeks later that he screwed up the courage to talk to Day, and was both amazed and relieved to learn that Day had seen the phantom train too.

In June of that same year, Day was again working as a fireman aboard another train heading for Lethbridge. Jim Nicholson, a friend of Twohey's, was the engineer driving the train that night. And to Day's horror, in almost the exact same spot just a few kilometres outside Medicine Hat, the ghost train reappeared. Once again, its headlight grew brighter and its whistle sounded louder as it approached, and once again it swerved off just in time to avoid a deadly collision. Day said nothing to Nicholson about his second near-crash with a train that couldn't possibly exist, but he began to wonder if he, like Twohey, should take a break from the rails.

It was just by chance that Day was given a yard assignment in Medicine Hat on July 8, 1908. That's where he was when he and other workers got some terrible news about a derailment just a few kilometres outside town. A passenger train travelling east had been nearly two hours late leaving Lethbridge. This was a vital piece of information for the engineer driving a locomotive south to Dunmore Junction, to pick up the luxury cars of the Spokane Flyer. If he had paid attention to the Lethbridge train's new expected arrival time in Medicine Hat, he would have delayed his train's departure from the Hat. But somehow he missed that information, and his error proved deadly. The two locomotives met headlong, killing seven members of the trains' crews and two passengers.

When more details about the terrible accident reached the rail yards, Gus Day's mind was sent reeling, first with grief and then with horror. He was grief-stricken when he heard that the crash had claimed the lives of four of his fellow workers. Two had been good friends — Bob Twohey and Jim Nicholson. Twohey had been the engineer on the train from Lethbridge and Nicholson had been the other locomotive's engineer. Day was also horrified to learn that the crash had happened in the very same place as the two earlier encounters with the ghost train.

THE WOMAN AT THE WINDOW

Regina, Saskatchewan

The house at 1800 College Avenue in Regina is at the east end of a row of century-old buildings that the city would like to see preserved. But the house doesn't just capture the flavour of Regina's architectural past. If you believe many of the stories about the place, it also appears to have captured a spirit from the past — a ghost named Rose.

Over the years, there were reports of Rose being spotted looking out from windows and drifting along hallways upstairs. She was also blamed for turning lights on and off, and for mysteriously breaking into song. Back in the late 1990s, a man named Trevor Lein moved into the house. After three years, he converted his home into a popular spot called Magellan's Global Coffee House, which he ran for another three years.

During his six years in the building, Lein kept an eye out for Rose, but he never encountered her. No one in the Sneath family had met her either, and they had lived there from the 1920s to the 1980s. Lein found this out when he decided to investigate various stories about a woman dying in the house, and learned that they weren't true. No one drowned in a water tank on the property; it never had a cistern. A nanny rumoured to have killed herself by taking a dive out a third-floor window had, in reality, moved on to enjoy life in Calgary. And there had never been a serious fire in the house, so no one had burned to death there either — another possible explanation given for Rose's haunting presence.

But one worker at the coffee house didn't really care what the ghost's name was, or why it might call 1800 College Avenue home. All she knew was that she had seen it three times — a mysterious woman in a wedding dress. And once, much to her shock, the bride had walked past a window overlooking the street — a window *on the second floor.*

1800 College Avenue

Another staff member was upset when she was alone in the kitchen and the dough mixer turned itself on. And another woman waitressing there had an alarming story to tell. She was making her way toward the tables when someone began to move toward her. Closer and closer the person came — directly in her path — until it passed right through her. The terrified waitress reported what had happened, and then promptly quit her job, hurrying out of Magellan's without ever looking back.

By 2006 the building was home to a computer-related business, and no one was publicly reporting any eerie encounters there. But there are still a few people in Regina who scan the upper floors as they pass in front of 1800 College Avenue — just in case the spectre of a woman is looking down on them.

THE TALKING STATUE

Burlington, Ontario

An eighty-five-year-old bronze statue of a World War I soldier stands atop a granite cenotaph beside Burlington's City Hall. The statue is similar to many others erected across the country. Together with other monuments and plaques bearing the names of members of Canada's war dead, they are often the focus of special ceremonies held each year on November 11 — Remembrance Day.

However, there were times when some of the people who gathered near the Burlington statue to honour the sacrifices of war found themselves paying more attention to the statue than the ceremonies. But that's understandable. Who wouldn't be distracted by seeing a statue move its hands or by hearing it speak?

Stories about the statue being haunted date back to

before the end of World War II. And the stories have followed it on its moves from Lakeside Park overlooking
Burlington Bay to a traffic island on Lakeshore Boulevard
and — after major additions to City Hall were completed
in 1986 — to the new civic square on Brant Street.

Over the years, in each location, as people stood in
silence around the statue on Remembrance Day, they
reported hearing the sounds of sergeants giving orders
and soldiers marching. Several times individuals heard

A ghostly mist surrounds the monument.

one particular voice calling out, "My name is Alfred." That
voice seemed to be coming from the statue. A few others
heard the mysterious voice add, "I lived a hero and I died
a hero." But perhaps most disturbing of all are the reports

that the bronze soldier shifts his hands as he grips the barrel of the rifle on which he leans, that his lips move and that, every now and then, he opens his eyes.

Among the names of the war dead listed on the Burlington cenotaph is that of Alfred Edward Johnson. Veterans Affairs Canada's records indicate that a soldier by that name died in action on August 19, 1942. Johnson, from Burlington, was one of one hundred and ninety-seven members of the Royal Hamilton Light Infantry brigade who were hit by German machine-gun fire as they stormed the main beach at Dieppe, France, on that date. His body, along with those of his brave comrades, is buried in the Dieppe Canadian War Cemetery far away in France.

Some local residents think that it is Johnson's ghost that haunts the statue on the civic square — and not just during memorial services. Rumour has it that the bronze soldier also moves at a time when many other spectres make appearances — under cover of darkness, at the midnight hour.

A GHOST IN THE AISLE

Calgary, Alberta

Years ago, a ghostly soldier similar to the bronze figure standing in Burlington's civic square made several appearances in Calgary — in the theatre at that city's Centennial Planetarium, now part of the Telus World of Science complex.

Sam, as the phantom came to be known, was dressed in the uniform of a World War I soldier. He would suddenly materialize in the theatre, walk around for a period of time, then quickly disappear as mysteriously as he had arrived. Staff and visitors alike reported seeing him, and some spoke of him following them for a few seconds. Others simply felt his presence as spots in the building became unusually chilly, and a few people smelled the scent of his shaving lotion.

It's been a long time since Sam was last spotted at the planetarium, but some of the staff who used to work there remember him fondly, and not with fear. However, a few other workers didn't wait around for the phantom soldier to stop making his spooky appearances. They bid him a not-so-fond farewell, quitting their jobs and finding employment elsewhere in a less scary, ghost-free environment.

THE PHANTOMS OF THE OPERA HOUSE

Orillia, Ontario

No one has seen the ghosts that haunt the Gordon Lightfoot Auditorium at the century-old Opera House in Orillia. Unlike Sam at the planetarium theatre in Calgary, these spirits prefer to remain invisible. But they don't remain silent.

One loves to play the grand piano. No one knows whether it's male or female — but every now and then, when the auditorium is empty, its haunting tunes fill the air. Its presence has frustrated technical staff who have heard the melodies — usually sad ones — drifting toward them as they work elsewhere in the building. No matter how quickly they rush into the auditorium to catch the piano-playing culprit, the music stops the instant they show up, and they never find anyone seated at the instrument on stage. A few workers have been upset enough by their encounters with the invisible keyboard player that they avoid being alone in the place, especially late at night, a time the phantom prefers for giving its performances.

There have been reports of other spooky spectres performing in the auditorium late at night. Again, the performers were invisible, but they definitely weren't quiet. A blast of cold air coming from the orchestra pit announced their presence, followed by the sounds of laughter, clapping, and shouts of "Bravo!" It's as if an invisible theatre troupe were taking a curtain call before a very appreciative audience. But there were no actors on stage, and the seats where the applauding audience should be were all empty.

The Orillia Opera House

A GHOSTLY GUEST APPEARANCE

Georgetown, Prince Edward Island

The ghost who haunts another theatre, this time in Georgetown, P.E.I., doesn't mind being seen.

He inhabited the historic town hall — which became the Kings Theatre — before it suffered a serious fire in 1983. And he continued to reveal himself in the Kings Playhouse that rose from its ashes a few years later.

Like Sam, the Calgary ghost haunting the planetarium theatre, he's been given a name — Captain George. And he's a bit of a prankster. Wearing an old-fashioned military officer's greatcoat and carrying a lantern, he suddenly appears on stage or behind the scenes, leaving both crews and actors feeling more than a little uneasy. He's also been known to upset a few theatre-goers by briefly gripping their ankles.

Managers at the theatre finally decided to take a firm but friendly approach to dealing with Captain George. They reserved a seat specifically for him — hoping that he'd stay put in it instead of roaming around disturbing people, especially during performances.

If only he would . . .

DEATH AT THE MILL

Manotick, Ontario

Joseph Merrill Currier was a self-made man. Born in Vermont in 1820, he moved to the Ottawa Valley when he was seventeen, and found a job as a lower-level employee of a lumber company. Within a few years he had worked his way up to the position of manager of three different lumber firms, and by the late 1840s, he had earned a reputation around the Ottawa area as a savvy businessman. In the 1850s he and another successful lumberman, Moss Kent Dickinson, became partners, building a large sawmill and then a gristmill for grinding grain on the Rideau River at Manotick, Canada West.

But Currier's personal life didn't follow the same successful path. In 1855 scarlet fever claimed the lives of his children. Three years later, his wife, Christina, died. So he couldn't believe his good fortune when in 1860, while vacationing on Lake George in New York State, he met a beautiful young woman who seemed to be interested in him. Anne Crosby was half Currier's age, but that difference didn't stop the couple from falling in love, and they were married in January of 1861. After honeymooning in the United States for a month, Currier brought his bride back to Ottawa.

Currier was proud of his accomplishments. He was especially proud of the flour mill he and Dickinson had built at Manotick. Business was booming there, and a thriving village was taking shape around it. The mill had begun operating in 1860, and its first anniversary was coming up, so Currier thought a visit there would be a great way to introduce Anne to friends in the area and to show off the mill to her. However, early on in the couple's visit, tragedy struck.

Currier had walked Anne around the property, pointing out to her how water flowing over a dam on the river powered the machinery that turned the large stones grinding wheat into flour. Then it was time to tour the four-storey stone building itself. When they reached the second floor where the millstones were turning, Anne's long skirt and petticoat got caught in the revolving mechanism that drove the stones. In an instant she was thrown violently against a large support pillar, and slumped to the floor, bleeding. Horrified, Currier ran to her, but there was nothing he could do. His beautiful wife was dead.

Currier wanted nothing to do with the mill after that. He would never again enter the room where bloodstains from the horrifying accident remained permanently soaked into the wooden pillar, and he would never return to Manotick. But it appears that his bride — or more specifically, her spirit — never left.

Over the years since Anne's death, several people have reported seeing a beautiful young woman in a long dress looking out of a second-floor window at the mill. Others have been frightened to hear blood-curdling screams coming from the mill at night when no one was there.

Watson's Mill, as it's now known, was bought and restored by the Rideau Valley Conservation Authority in the 1970s, and has become a popular tourist attraction. It's one of a few gristmills that are still operating in Ontario. But some visitors have felt very uncomfortable, especially when they are on the second floor. They start to shiver and feel cold there even on scorching hot summer days, and they have a sense that someone is watching them and wishes they would leave. Many believe that that someone is Anne — her spirit trapped forever where she met such a horrible fate. Perhaps she is wishing she could leave too.

Watson's Mill at night

Peace at Last

Joseph Currier married again, seven years after Anne died. His third wife was Hannah Wright, from Hull, Quebec. Hoping to start life afresh, he built a fine new home for Hannah, who came from a well-off family used to entertaining in a grand style.

The limestone mansion sat on a large tree-covered lot overlooking the Ottawa River. Currier called the place Gorffwysfa, a Welsh word meaning a peaceful place. He lived there until his death in 1884, and Hannah stayed on in Gorffwysfa until she died in 1901.

The stately house still stands in Ottawa, and Canadians like to think that the families who have lived there over the past many years have indeed found it to be a peaceful place. Its address? 24 Sussex Drive — the official home of Canada's prime ministers since 1951.

A DISTURBING GUEST

Winnipeg, Manitoba

The impressive-looking building at 335 Donald Street just north of Portage Avenue in Winnipeg was built in 1895. Known as the old Masonic Temple, it was the headquarters for local lodges, or branches, of the Masonic Order, a somewhat secretive men's organization whose members pledge loyalty to each other and support efforts to help others in the community.

In 1969, not long after the Masons sold it, the building became home to a Mother Tucker's Restaurant and, although the owner of the restaurant chain denied it, it was also home to a ghost. One server working there in August of 1979 actually saw the ghost for a few seconds. The apparition was that of a tall young man in a top hat and old-fashioned dress coat standing off to one side of the main room. But several other staff members who encountered the unusual restaurant guest usually just heard it or saw signs that it had been moving around the place.

After the restaurant closed, servers would tidy up and set the tables so they would be ready for the next day's customers. But some mornings when they returned, they would find serviettes wrinkled up, salt and pepper shakers knocked over, sugar spilt, and knives and forks lying in disarray. As one waiter put it, the dining room looked as if someone had had a party there in the middle of the night. Tom Sacco, the manager at the time, reported that he and others would occasionally hear mysterious footsteps moving around overhead, even though he had just done a security check of the upper floors before locking up. One night, sounds of a vicious argument were also heard coming from an empty room upstairs.

Generally speaking, though, staff at Mother Tucker's felt they could put up with the mysterious presence that seemed to prefer haunting the upper floors. They just did not want to be alone with it, especially not at night, after closing time.

A WRAITH ON THE WARD

Vancouver, British Columbia

At the time — back in the mid-1970s — officials at
Vancouver General Hospital thought it would be best if the
public didn't know the hospital's burn unit might be
haunted. They were probably right. After all, knowing that
a ghost could be helping out with their nursing care might
not be such a comforting thought for most patients suffering from very serious burns. But if nurses were right
about identifying him, the unit's ghost would have been
very sympathetic toward their suffering. In life, he had
himself spent three agonizing months bravely fighting to
recover from horrible burns over much of his body.

The young man, referred to here as Jim — his real
name was never publicly associated with the haunting —
was one of sixteen workers seriously injured in a major

explosion and fire in a grain elevator at the Burrard dock facilities in October 1975. Jim's injuries were the most serious. He was listed in critical condition and wasn't expected to survive. But, isolated in Room 415 to reduce the chance of infection, Jim somehow found the will to live and to cope with the excruciating pain caused by his third-degree burns. However, over the next several weeks his heroic battle sapped his strength, and three months after the fire he died.

Nurses who had cared for Jim were very sad when he died, but in the weeks and months following his death they began to think his spirit lived on in the burn unit, and not just in their tender memories of him. When some of them entered Room 415 to check on a patient, they began to feel that another invisible presence had entered with them. When nurse Denny Conrad was in the room one day getting it ready for the arrival of a new patient, he thought another staff member had followed him in carrying a tray of bandages. But when he turned around the tray fell, and there was no one else there. That incident disturbed Conrad; he didn't like the idea of being in the same room as a ghost, even if it was Jim's. Another nurse who went into 415 when no patient was there heard sounds of deep breathing coming from the empty bed, and saw the sheets move as if a patient were tossing and turning.

There were also reports of Jim visiting burn victims on the ward. One critically ill woman mentioned she'd just had a visit from a kindly young man she didn't know. The nurse was surprised to hear this since, as with Jim, the woman was being kept in isolation and was only allowed visits from members of her immediate family. Another time, a patient in Room 413 beside Jim's old room asked a nurse to pass along his thanks to the nice young doctor who had spent time with him the night before, helping him cope with his pain. The nurse was fairly certain no doctor had been on the ward then, but she checked the records to make sure and saw that she was right. Curious, she went back and asked the patient to describe what the doctor had looked like. She wasn't all that surprised when the patient described a man who looked just like Jim. However, she didn't tell the patient what she was thinking — that Jim's ghost had been making his rounds.

Most of the burn unit staff at the time felt that Jim's spirit was trying to be helpful when it actually made an appearance. Those occurrences were disturbing, but tolerable. However, some other ghostly activities were upsetting and even disruptive at times. Icy blasts of air would suddenly fill Room 415. Taps opened and the toilet flushed when the bathroom was empty, and the lights often switched on and off on their own. The signal to call for a nurse's assistance would also be triggered when no patient was in the room. Some people thought that these eerie encounters were Jim's way of letting them know he was still there.

Shortly before the burn unit was moved to another wing during the hospital's expansion, the unsettling incidents stopped. Nurses who had cared for Jim hoped that meant he had found pain-free rest at last.

THE DARK LADY

Hamilton, Ontario

The old Custom House at 51 Stuart Street in the north end of Hamilton is a magnificent stone building that is considered a national historic site. Opened in 1860, it was designed to look like many official buildings and museums constructed in Italy in the nineteenth century. It was built to house government workers who kept track of goods moving in and out of the city's busy port on Lake Ontario, and who collected duties, or special taxes, on many imported products.

Customs officials moved out in 1887 and, over the next hundred or so years, the building had many different owners and tenants. It became a temporary elementary school, a branch of the YWCA, a rooming house, a shelter for the homeless, several workplaces including factories that made vinegar, woollen yarn and pasta, a martial arts academy and a computer company. In the late 1980s the Ontario government spent a lot of money to help the karate school renovate and restore the building. In 1995 the current owner — the Ontario Workers Arts and Heritage Centre — bought it, using it to focus on the history and cultural contributions of Canadian working-class men and women. In 2001 the centre changed its name to the Workers Arts and Heritage Centre.

But while the owners and uses of the Custom House changed many times over the course of its colourful history, one thing stayed the same — the claim that the stately stone building was haunted by a ghost known as The Lady in Black, or The Dark Lady.

The Dark Lady is said to live in the basement of 51 Stuart Street, but she seems to move around a lot. There have been reported sightings of a beautiful woman appearing in a top-floor window of the building. However, a much older woman all dressed in black has also appeared in the place. In one instance decades ago, a worker named Mr. Hanman saw just the shadowy shape of a woman gliding along a wall. Years later, during the restoration, one member of the construction crew saw The Black Lady clearly and got a sense that she was upset by the changes going on around her, especially plans to move the mantelpiece around one fireplace. Perhaps that's why she kept moving their tools after they went home for the day, and why she may have caused a major roof leak that flooded several rooms soon after the mantel was moved. Several workers also experienced a very strange, uncomfortable sensation and a blast of frigid air when they worked in the basement.

At least two stories offer a possible explanation for the

tragic figure's lingering presence in the Custom House. One says that she's the ghost of an unidentified immigrant who died on a ship that arrived in Hamilton and whose body was buried in the basement. Legend has her roaming the place for all these years as she waits for her lover to join her in Canada. Another tale that circulated years

A staircase leading to the basement of the Custom House

ago was about a ship's captain who murdered his wife and buried her there after she found out that he had a girl-friend and demanded that he end the affair. There seems to be no evidence backing up either possibility.

However, evidence that The Dark Lady has been around for a very long time may be found in a ballad by Hamiltonian Alexander Wingfield that was published in 1873. Titled "The Woman in Black," the poem begins with a specific reference to what the ghost wore.

> *The ghosts — long ago — used to dress in pure white,*
> *Now they're got on a different track,*
> *For the Hamilton Ghost seems to take a delight*
> *To stroll 'round the city in black.*

Wingfield then goes on to tell how frightened a police-man was when he suddenly encountered the black-garbed spectre while walking the beat near the Custom House one night.

> *A "Peeler," who met her, turned blue with affright*
> *And in terror he clung to a post;*
> *His hair (once a carroty red) has turned white,*
> *Since the moment he looked on the ghost.*

Wingfield ends the poem rather dramatically a few verses later, telling of how the poor officer was found frozen with fear at 2 a.m., still clinging to the lamppost. But according to another earlier verse, his terror was understandable. The apparition he saw was much more horrifying than the one usually seen at the Custom House.

Her breath seemed as hot as a furnace; besides,
It smelt strongly of sulphur and gin,
Two horns (a yard long) stuck straight out of her head,
And her hoofs made great clatter and din.

That ghost sounds absolutely demonic. Fortunately for those who've spotted the ghostly woman in black at 51 Stuart Street since that poem was published, the spectre they've seen doesn't smell of sulphur and gin, and she doesn't have horns or hoofs.

THE MAYBE GHOST

Orwell River, Prince Edward Island

James Hayden Fletcher didn't believe in ghosts. As a young boy growing up in a small community at the mouth of the Orwell River about twenty-five kilometres east of Charlottetown, P.E.I., he and his siblings loved hearing the spooky stories that workers at his father's sawmill would tell as they sat around the fireplace at the end of the day. The stories filled them all with a delicious mix of excitement and fear.

When he grew up, Fletcher was a little disappointed, but very relieved, to find out that most of those tales were grounded, not in facts, but in Irish and Scottish superstitions, and he stopped believing in ghosts. He even went so far as to try to convince friends and neighbours who did that they were foolish to do so.

Still, in an article titled "The Ghost Story" published in *The Prince Edward Island Magazine* in 1900 when he was about sixty, Fletcher admitted that those scary stories still had an impact on him as a non-believing adult. He confessed that "whenever I got into a suspicious place after dark, I always looked over my shoulder to make sure that no unnatural visitor was crawling on me from behind."

So it didn't come as a surprise that, as a young man, he started feeling very nervous walking home from the blacksmith's shop after dark one night, especially when he realized he would have to pass by an old graveyard. He tried to focus on the road ahead, but when he came to the cemetery gate, he couldn't resist turning toward it. He immediately wished he hadn't.

Decades later, Fletcher still remembered vividly what he saw that night — a mysterious, tall, white figure. In the "Ghost Story" article, he wrote about how he felt at that moment. "In spite of my philosophy, I felt my hat rise from my head . . . I looked out into the darkness again and saw it move! . . . There was no mistake about it — the spectre continued to move! . . . It slowly began to advance toward me. It gradually appeared to grow taller and whiter."

Fletcher was terrified, but he decided not to run, just in case the ghostly figure was the spirit of a close friend who wanted to communicate with him — a strange thought for someone who didn't believe in ghosts. Instead he decided to speak to it. "How do you do?" he asked, and was incredibly relieved to hear a human voice answer, "Well. Thank the Lord." Fletcher recalled, "It was the most welcome sound I ever heard, and yet I became so weak I could scarcely walk."

But walk Fletcher did, as quickly as he could, not lingering to chat with the white-robed figure, whom he thought he recognized as an old fellow from New Perth known as "Crazy Donald Gordon." Gordon had apparently become mentally ill in his old age, and had started wearing strange robes and performing bizarre religious rituals. Fletcher assumed Gordon had been saying prayers for the dead in the graveyard. Nevertheless, he readily admitted that nothing he had ever seen in his whole life had ever frightened him so badly as the appearance of the white-robed man in the cemetery.

But could Fletcher's first impression — that a ghost was moving toward him — have been correct? After all, he did mention in his article that Gordon had "scarcely ever been seen before in the vicinity of Orwell." He also referred to the man as a "patriarch," the head of a large family. A few old records point to the possibility that one Donald Gordon, who fathered many children, may have already been *dead* when Fletcher walked past the graveyard. Of course, records can be incorrect or incomplete. But maybe they weren't. Maybe Fletcher, the man who didn't believe in ghosts, had very good reason to be afraid that night.

HAUNTED CANADA

True Ghost Stories

This collection of chilling true ghost stories
from all across Canada will send shivers down
your spine. From poltergeists who terrorize
hunters in a remote cabin to a man who
gets frightened to death in a graveyard, prepare
yourself to be haunted!

Winner of the Diamond Willow Award

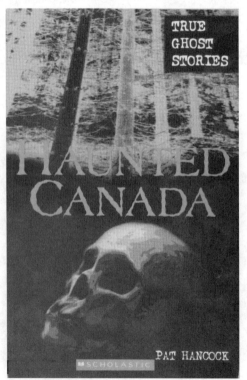

ISBN 978-0-7791-1410-8

HAUNTED CANADA
True Tales of Terror

These terrifying true tales from all parts of Canada will chill you to the bone. Strange fires break out, serpents rise from the waves, and giant beasts lumber through the trees. Ghostly forms drift by and eerie disks lower silently from the sky. Get set for some haunting experiences!

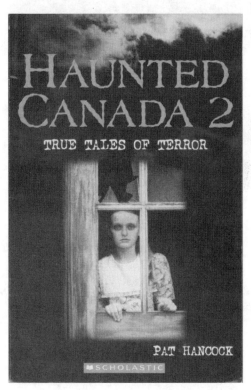

ISBN 978-0-439-96122-6